by the Bishop of London

This story, about a unique bequest, begins in 1348 at a time
when much of Europe was in the grip of the horror of the Black Death.
In squalid urban areas as many as half the population perished;
certainly in the dense confines of fourteenth century London
the figure may well have been higher.

Margaret Troke's highly readable account traces the history
of the will made by John Thavie, armourer and affluent citizen of London,
in September 1348, which included a bequest to the Rector
and Churchwardens that was to provide support to maintain the Parish
Church of St Andrew Holborn in perpetuity, a role
which it continues to fill 650 years on. The story is told in the context
of contemporary life and historical events over seven centuries.

The Thavie endowment is a remarkable survivor as many
such bequests were confiscated during the Reformation. That it continues
to thrive to this day is a testimony to the good husbandry
and diligence of generations of Rectors, Vicars and Churchwardens
of St Andrew Holborn and their fellow trustees. Their efforts are evident
in the well-maintained Wren Guild Church that still commands
the attention of travellers entering the City of London from the west
as it did in 1348.

I commend this book to you. Not only does it tell
a fascinating story but it also speaks loudly and clearly about the faith
of many ordinary men and women from John Thavie
onward who, through their firm commitment to our Lord, contributed
down the ages towards the cause of maintaining
the Church of St Andrew Holborn as a place of worship.
That St Andrews still fulfils this purpose
for local residents and city workers, and, in addition serves
as headquarters for the Royal College of Organists and administrative
centre for the Archdeaconry of Hackney and various charities,
is witness to the ongoing success of their efforts.

+ *Richard Londin :*

CHAPTER ONE

The Legacy

I. JOHN TAVY (THAVIE)

In 1348, on the Thursday before the Feast of St. Gregory the Pope, John Tavy, Armurer, made his will. Like many other pious and affluent parishioners of St. Andrew's in medieval times, he left land and property to the Church, the income from which was to provide `one fit chaplain` to pray for his soul and that of his wife Alice. Charitably, the souls of `all the faithful departed this life` were to be included in these prayers.

These chantry lands and bequests - and St. Andrew's had many - were all confiscated by the Crown two hundred years later at the time of the Reformation, so John Tavy would have become just one more name on a long list of forgotten benefactors if it had not been for the last clause in his will. "Also I bequeath all that tenement wherein I inhabit, with the three shops which I lately purchased of William Passmore, after the decease of the aforesaid Alice my wife for (the supporting) the fabric of the Church of St. Andrew in Holborn ("ad fabricationem ecclesiae")".

This last clause could not be interpreted by the Crown Commissioners of Edward VI as being for 'superstitious purposes' - the usual excuse - so now, six hundred and fifty years later, John Tavy's gift still maintains the Church and provides for the administration of what is known as the St. Andrew Church Foundation

John Tavy, (sometimes Tavey, Thavey, Thavie or Tany), 'Armurer', must have been an important member of the community. Unfortunately, no church records from the fourteenth century have survived, and the early records of the Craft Guild were destroyed in the Great Fire of 1666, so the only sources of information available are the Hustings Rolls and the charters granted to the City Guilds by the King.

We know that John Thavie was a member of the Guild of St. George of the Armourers, whose first charter was granted in 1322. In the Articles of the Armourers, made at the Hustings of Common Pleas in the same year, he is named as one of the 27 members of the Guild who, in the presence of the Mayor and Sheriffs of the City agreed 'for the common profit, that henceforth armour made for sale in the City should be good and fit'. From the detailed description that follows, of materials to be used and procedures to be adopted, it is clear that two crafts were involved in the making of armour. The first was that of the brazier or blacksmith, and the second was the craft of linen-armourer. They were to separate five years later.

John Thavie was a linen-armourer. He made the padded tunics or gambesons worn under, or even without, armour. These tunics had to be strong enough to resist ordinary sword-cuts, so it could be a matter of life or death if standards were not strictly maintained. It was equally important that the covered helmets, called basnets, should give adequate protection. For this reason, it was agreed that - "no Smith shall cover any basnet himself for sale, but shall sell them out of his hand quite new and uncovered and they shall remain uncovered until they have been seen by the four (members of the Guild) who have been sworn or by two of them, whether they be fit for covering or not".

John Thavie was one of the four 'sworn men', which you could say made him a kind of medieval trading standards officer. Regular and random checks were made and anyone found with sub-standard armour for sale was taken before the Mayor and Aldermen for judgement.

THE NEW GUILD

In 1327 the Guild of Taylors and Linen Armourers was granted its first charter by Edward III. This had developed from an earlier religious fraternity (John the Baptist). In the 'Mistery of Taylors and Linen Armourers elected and sworn for the government and instruction of the same', John Thavie is named as one of 21 members of the new Guild. (Mistery here is simply another word for craft). The oath is interesting:

"Ye shall swear that ye shall wele and treuly ov'see the Craft whereof ye be chosen Wardeyns for the yeere. All the defaults ye shall wele and treuly presente sparyng noo man for favour, ne grevyng noo persone for hate, noo doo nether to noo thing that shalbe ayenst the state, peas, and profite of our Sovereyn Lord the Kinge or to the Citie. So help you God and all Seyntes."

The social and welfare aspect of Guild membership was an important part of John Thavie's life. All members made a yearly contribution to a common fund that existed to help their fraternity in times of hardship or trouble. And trouble there was, sometimes. In the Calendar of Plea and Memoranda Rolls for 1338 there is an entry about Roger de la Tour, armourer, who was brought before the Mayor, Aldermen and Sheriffs by some inhabitants of Cheap(side) accused of being a common disturber of the peace and having assaulted Thomas de Kesteven. He was committed to prison, but subsequently mainprised by several other armourers including John Thavie. On referring to earlier notes, we found that the victim was also an armourer!

With regular social gatherings - the great annual pageant of the guilds at St. Paul's - mourning at each others' funerals - there was real community spirit here.

As well as the responsibilities of Guild membership, John Thavie would have had the welfare of his apprentices to consider. We know that they were housed at his inn or hostel - a sensible arrangement; apprenticeships were for several years, and a firm hand was needed. Not only did these lads have to be fed and clothed, but at a time when public brawling was a common occurrence among rival apprentice groups they had to be persuaded to behave themselves.

OTHER DUTIES

In his role as citizen and freeman of the City of London, John Thavie had other duties to perform. On at least three occasions in 1339 and 1340, he is mentioned as an official at the Coroner's Court, investigating 'deaths other than rightful deaths'. The first case was of William, son of John de Cublingtone (no cause given): the second was Alice Warde of Yorke, who had been stabbed in Faitoure's (Fetter's) Lane. The third involved John King, currour, who 'died suspiciously'. Yet another case concerning a stabbing after curfew describes John Thavie as a 'gude man of the Warde' when he was called as a good neighbour - (a character witness, perhaps?) to a servant of John de Norhampton.

FINAL DAYS

This 'gude man' became prosperous; all the armourers were kept very busy. Continuing sporadic war against France meant a continual demand for armour. Froissart reported that in 1346 when Edward III fought the Battle of Crecy on his way back to the coast after ravaging Normandy, he had 2,300 men-at-arms, 5,200 archers and 1,000 Welshmen under his command.

In midsummer 1348, the Sheriffs banned the holding of jousts and tournaments so much enjoyed by the people. They were to " betake themselves to the more serious exercise of arms (archery) for the safety of the realm against the King's enemies".

The exact date of John Thavie's death is not known, or how old he was, but the date of his will is significant. It was made at a time when the Black Death had reached London from Europe via Southampton and Bristol. As an importer of woollen cloth he would have had prior warning of this latest plague, and would have been well aware of the danger, for the mortality rate was high. It is estimated that between one third and one half of the population of England died in the following two years.

For us, John Thavie will remain a rather shadowy figure, in his long fur-collared robe and flat, pointed shoes, but we can be sure that at his funeral his coffin was covered by the beautifully embroidered Guild pall, and that it was followed by the Master and all the members of his fraternity in their fine livery. He was laid to rest in St Andrew's Church with all due ceremony.

II. THE CHURCH - 1348.

Rebuilding a church in the later style

(From a drawing belonging to the Society of Anriquaries)

In the fourteenth century, it seems that people were all determined to have their own local parish church. Fitzstephen wrote that there were 126 such churches in the City of London and the Liberties surrounding its walls. Not all of these were architecturally pleasing, or even solidly built. Many of them disappeared without trace after the Reformation.

There were also the palatial monastic establishments of the Whitefriars, Greyfriars, Blackfriars and Crutched Friars. The Cluniac order at Bermondsey on the south bank held the advowson or patronage of St. Andrew's at this time. These communities were by no means contemplative orders. In fact they had enormous influence on the daily lives of the people.

The focal point of all this religious activity was St.

Paul's, its lofty spire dominating the skyline. The members of all the parish churches gathered there on their particular Saint's Day, as did the fraternities of the various guilds. These processions and pageants must have been an impressive sight.

St. Andrew's was in a fortunate position. Already long-established - it was mentioned as a wooden structure in a statute of King Edgar in the tenth century; it stood at the top of Oldbourne Hill on the south side of what had been the main highway to the west since Roman times. Flete Street and the Strand were to become more important as a direct route to Westminster, but Holborn has been described as the first West End of London. It had many wealthy high profile residents in what was then a predominantly rural environment. The Church itself was surrounded on three sides by gardens, and the entrance was from Sho (Shoe) Lane.

To the east of the church, down the hill, was the Flete River crossed by Oldbourne bridge to Newgate, one of the seven entrances into the walled city.

To the south, Flete Street and the Strand was busily developing as the area of the early Inns of Court and of noblemens' mansions.

To the west, was John Thavie's 'mansion', a few shops, and Besville's Inn (an early Inn of Chancery). Beyond Besville's Inn was John Thavie's apprentices' inn, facing onto Faitoure's Lane.

On the north side of Oldbourne was Lord Furnival's property (later Furnival's Inn) and Lither (Leather) Lane, then open fields flanking the newly built palace and gardens of the Bishop of Ely. Across the bridge was the great Priory and hospital of St. Bartholomew. Between the Bishop's palace and the priory lay the famous Smoothfield (Smithfield), where a Horse Fair was held on Fridays, and jousts and tournaments took place.

A medieval priest in vestments for celebrating mass. Note the circular chasuble, worn over a white linen alb. The decorated panels are called the apparel.

(Drawing of a brass rubbing - Monkton Church)

So much for the location, but what of the church itself? The earliest tiny sketch of St. Andrew's is that on the Agas map of the sixteenth century, so we can only rely on later records for any detailed description. However, there are a few such ancient churches still in existence, most of them similar in construction, so we can say what it (probably) looked like. At this stage, it would have been a rectangular single-storey stone building, possibly thatched. About one hundred years old (Norman Gothic?), it had a single row of pointed windows. Consisting only of nave and chancel, a small belfry had been added in 1280, so there was at least one bell to summon people to the daily services, and to join St. Paul's and all the other parish churches in ringing the curfew at eight o'clock each evening. There were rules about being out after curfew, but at least no-one could plead ignorance of the time - the noise must have been deafening.

The bagpiper and the harpist.

(From a 14th century woodcarving, Christchurch Priory)

Walking into the church, one's first impressions would have been of brightness, light and the ever-present smell of incense. Brightness from the colourful painted frescoes round the walls - perhaps the lives of the saints - light from the many torches, candles and tapers burning, not only on and around the chancel altar, but on the three or four small altars or statues ranged against the walls.

In the main body of the church people might be standing or kneeling in prayer. The Rector (or one of his assistants) could be celebrating Mass, but at the same time other priests might be holding their own services at the small altars. These were chantry priests who were paid to pray for the souls of the dead.

On certain days too, there was probably a scribe (yet another priest) ready to write letters or copy documents for the largely illiterate parishioners. Nearly everyone attended church every day, so we can assume that St. Andrew's was a popular general meeting-place as well as a busy centre of devotion.

Attached to the church at this time there was also a Cluniac cell. It has been referred to as a small hospice, though it may have been the home of a friar living a hermit-like existence, depending on the alms of passers-by for food and sustenance. Parishioners quite liked having their own anchorite; contemporary writers observed that churchgoers derived satisfaction from hearing sounds of groaning and scourging coming from the cell. The louder the groans, the greater his rewards, presumably!

III. LIFE IN THE FOURTEENTH CENTURY.

The congregation of St. Andrew's in John Thavie's time included wealthy merchants, craftsmen, lawyers and nobles, but their apprentices and retainers, down to the humblest bondsmen, were also parishioners.

There was no official poor law, but rich people often left money 'for the poor of the parish', and the church distributed it. The church was without doubt the most powerful influence on the lives of ordinary people. It would continue to be so for the next two hundred years, though it would be increasingly criticised for corruption, and other misdeeds among the clergy.

Alan Ivimey, in his 'History of London', put it most succinctly when he described the church as a "Ministry of Health, a Ministry of Education and a Ministry of Labour, as well as the Board of Agriculture and Fisheries". Besides tending the sick, running schools, and feeding thousands of destitute people, monasteries took in frail elderly relatives, unmarried daughters considered to be past their 'sell-by date' and the mentally handicapped, all for a very small charge. They were the only hotels of the time, too.

Life was not exactly comfortable. The narrow muddy lanes of the City and its Liberties (with the exception of the few main highways) were not wide enough to take carts for the transport of goods; pack horses and donkeys were used.

Palaces, monasteries, churches, mansions and tiny cottages (one up, one down, and no mod. cons.) were huddled together in a haphazard way. The smaller homes were of wattle and daub construction, and consequently a great fire hazard. Larger establishments were required by law to provide a long ladder, a long-handled hook and rake to remove burning thatch, and chains to pull down the whole house if the fire threatened to spread. A barrel of water to be kept by the door completed these instructions.

Contemporary bye-laws made by the Wardemote tell us quite a lot about the worries and concerns of local inhabitants; the one headed 'Of Swine' for example. " No swine shall be found about the lanes or in the suburbs or in the fosse (ditch) of the said City. And if swine be found they may be killed by those who find them. And he who shall wish to feed a pig must feed it in his own house". Escaping pigs squealing along the lanes must have been quite a problem, to prompt this law. Also one hopes that "in his own house" meant in his own garden, for they all had gardens, however small. Nearly everyone kept a pig - salt pork was a welcome addition to their diet in winter.

The Wardemote regulated the ale supply, too. "Let every brewer and brewster sell the gallon of best ale at one penny halfpenny and not more, and that they brew as good ale, or better, as they were wont before the proclamation".

This bye-law needs no explanation. "Item. That no person throw straw, dust, dung or other refuse into the streets or lanes; but cause them to be taken by the rakers to the places ordained for receiving such dirt". In an Ordinance of the time, it appears that twelve carts, each with two horses, were kept at the City's expense for the removal of sewage and refuse. They worked at night when the streets were empty.

FUN   AND   GAMES

Processions, pageants, miracle plays, were all part of everyday life. People flocked to the displays of jousting and the special tournaments at Smithfield. Regrettably, they seemed to enjoy the spectacle of a poor wretch being pilloried almost as much, and were not above indulging   in audience participation. Crowds lined the streets when a condemned prisoner was taken up the hill outside St. Andrew's on the way from Newgate to Tyburn, and many followed, to witness the public executions.

Fitzstephen wrote:- "In the holidays all the summer the youths are exercised in leaping, dancing, shooting (archery), wrestling, casting the stone and practising their shields ... In winter, every holiday before dinner, the boars prepared for brawn (i.e. about to be killed for food) are set to fight, or else bulls and bears are baited".

Cock-fighting, cock-throwing and football were especially in season at Shrovetide; these continued to be popular in spite of attempts to ban them. Football was usually played in the streets - it was therefore a 'great nuisance', often ending in fights. Broken bones and other injuries were the inevitable result. The players were regarded as hooligans because of the unruly aggressive nature of the no-holds-barred game.

It is noticeable that there is only one mention of women and girls in this account. "And the maidens, one of them playing on the timbrel, danced and sang... for garlands hung athwart the streets". However, in 1348, one group of ladies, no doubt tired of being just a decorative addition to the crowd, dressed themselves in men's clothes (parti-coloured jerkins and hose, complete with daggers at their belts) and rode on horseback intending to take part in a tournament. The chronicler, Henry Knighton, then piously states, "But God, against these as against others, sent heavy rain, thunder and lightning, and defeated their purpose with divers extraordinary tempests".

IV. THAVIE'S INN

Before leaving 1348, one important fact must be established. Contrary to popular belief, the Thavie's Inn of to-day is not and never was connected with John Tavy or Thavie.

E. Williams, in his classic work "Early Holborn and the Legal Quarters", published in 1927, explained it very clearly.

> "Amongst the ancient gifts of property to the Church of St. Andrew was one arising from Besvile's Inn, afterwards Davy's Inn and now Thavie's Inn. John de Besvile died in 1353, leaving his property in Holborn to certain Clerks of the Chancery then occupying it, with remainder to the said Church. The houses forming the frontage of his Inn lay immediately to the west of the church; but it so happened that on the other side of them, other houses had also been bequeathed to the said church, in reversion, by John Tavy, an armourer, together with an Inn where apprentices were lodged, forming afterwards part of Mirfields Inn and now known as Bartletts Buildings. In after years Besvile's gift was forgotten and his houses were erroneously assumed to form part of the gift of John Tavy".

So why Davy's Inn, then Thavie's Inn? John Davy died 50 years after John Tavy; he also left chantry money to the church. The confusion arose, we believe, when John Davy moved into Besvile's Inn from his property on the north side of Holborn, probably as Master or Sergeant (he never owned it) and the Inn then took his name, as often happened. Add to this the fact that the names Davy and Tavy or Thavie were interchangeable in those days of arbitrary spelling and it is easy to see how this mistake happened and was perpetuated for so long.

The law firm of Pontifex, Pitt, who managed the Thavie Estate in the nineteenth century actually inserted "in law" in brackets after the word 'apprentices' in their office transcript of John Tavy's will. Of course they were not apprentices at law, they were his own apprentice armourers.

CHAPTER TWO

Changes and Improvements

I. THE CHURCH 1348-1547

During the next two hundred years, the simple building already described underwent many changes and improvements thanks to the generosity of St. Andrew's parishioners. In 1360 a chapel to St. John the Baptist was built, and the following year two bequests provided St. John's window (6 marks) and St. John's door (1 mark).

By 1534, 5 altars are mentioned, but not all of these had become chapels, like the ones to St. John and St. Syth.

The Church continued to grow in size and importance, and when the charismatic Gilbert Worthington became Rector in 1439 it was decided to rebuild the church. Thomas Bentley (of whom more later) records that...

> "ye steeple of ye church of St. Andrew's that now is was begun to
> be buylded and ye old Steeple puled down in ye xxv yere of King
> Henry the Sixt and made up so that ye Bells were fyrst going up
> therein and ronge in ye xxxv yere of ye sayd K.Henry ye VI, but
> that ye same was not now fully finished in that Kings dayes untill
> ye vii or viii yere of King Edward ye fourth".

Bentley even gives us the names and weights of the bells.

This bell tower can still be seen in the church today, or rather the inside of it, in the Lady Chapel. Poor Gilbert Worthington - the rebuilding had hardly begun when he died, and was buried at his own request at the door of the chancel (In hostis cancelli).

Opposite: The Bell Tower of St Andrew's. The interior of which dates from the 15th century

THE NEW CHURCH

During the 22 years of rebuilding, north and south aisles were added; also a vestry, for in 1448 an amount of £6.10s. was recorded for its window. The church having been enlarged, the roof was raised and a second row of windows added, to let in more light. Again, in 1511, we are told that "the middle roof of the body of the church was new made", at a cost of £40.

In 1517 an organ loft was built and a "little organ" installed for £6. A wooden door and porch were built on the north side of the church. (It was to be replaced later- in 1584- by the old stone doorway from the original entrance on the south side, which was then "stopped up").   By 1526 the roof of the steeple had to be replaced, and the bells re-hung.

Now St. Andrew's was a church that for two hundred years had been enlarged and beautified. There was the main altar in the chancel, and a carved wooden rood screen and loft, complete with cross. There were several chantry chapels: the Guild Chapels to St. Syth, and St. John(with St. Christopher). There was also the private chapel of the Earl of Southampton by 1545, when Henry Wriothesley (later the second Earl), was baptised. The first Earl, Lord Chancellor of England, was buried here in 1550, though his body was later transferred to Titchfield.

The Resurrection.
c.1400, alabaster, height 43.3 cm.
London, Victoria and Albert Museum.

A powerful image of the risen Christ,
and a fine rendering also of the dress of an
infantry man of the late 14th century.

The private chapels and altars were probably ranged against the walls of the north and south aisles, and (on a slightly raised floor section?) in the middle of the nave, rows of carved pews on either side of a central aisle.

There were statues of St. Andrew and of the Virgin Mary, with a standing font nearby.

A church grammar school had been founded in the reign of Henry VI, and with the advent of the printing press, books were now available. By the end of this period, the church had acquired an Antiphonal, seven Mass books, five collections of psalms for singing, a book of legends of Saints, one ordinal or priest's manual, six psalters and five Processionals (litanies, hymns and prayers). There was also the Great English Bible of 1539 (required by law) and a translation of Erasmus's 'Commentary on the Gospels'.

II. PEOPLE, 1348 - 1547

Thomas Bentley is full of praise for "ye great devocon and zeal of ye people in old tyme towards ye hous of ye Lord ye Church" in the rebuilding and refurbishing carried out in the fifteenth and early sixteenth centuries. He names 36 of them, including eight Royal Justices, as well as the Inns of Court and Chancery, who were "great benefactors yerely for the most part".

We know that the Leat or Wardemote Inquests "at theyr syttings" gave money for the maintenance of the church "even then when it had most Landerents". Henry VII gave a legacy of 20 shillings and two torches to the church, which was paid by Henry VIII in the first year of his reign.

The churchwardens were responsible for repairing the church wall, and they "sett or sowed hemp in the garden, for the which, they like good husbands made money to the use of the church". They also kept the garden "to ye use of ye parishe for them to walk and recreat them selves in".

Money for the 'churchworks', as Bentley calls them, was also obtained by plays, shooting matches, 'ales' or drinkings (the barrels of ale were donated). Sundays and other holy days were marked by 'gatherings', at which the churchwardens rattled their alms dishes.

The parish priest was found guilty of offending his churchwardens and was fined 3s. and 4d.: he was also fined 4d. for "suffering a cart to come into ye Churchyard to ye parsonage house". All these contributions were duly noted in the churchwardens' accounts. Perhaps the most interesting entry is a description of the 5-day entertainment at Ely Palace in 1531, which the King attended, and for which the churchwardens lent the Church Plate, - for a fee, of course.

But by the end of the fifteenth century, towns and cities were spreading beyond the confines of their walls, and as Trevelyan puts it "National control and individual initiative were taking the place of the corporate spirit of town and guild." Then in 1531 came "the crash of monastic masonry resounding through the land" instigated by Henry VIII. The dissolution of the monastic orders was welcomed by many, because of the changing attitudes of people towards religion, life and society. The general feeling towards monks and friars was one of hostility and resentment. Their enormous wealth and lack of spiritual integrity was seen as an abuse of privilege. As Stow says "We are now come to the period when our streets were no longer to be crowded with monks and friars of various orders walking with their heads shaven and bare, with long beards, and a rosary hanging at their girdles". The nobility and gentry were said to be ' affronted in the streets' by Cardinals with their retinues of followers.

The new 'Defender of the Faith' had taken over, and Papal authority was repudiated. The sale of the monastic lands satisfied Henry for a time, but towards the end of his life he turned his attention to parish churches and their charities.

CHAPTER THREE

The Later Tudor and Stuart Years

I. THE CHURCH 1547-1687

Henry VIII died; Protestants triumphed under the boy King Edward VI, and the seizure of chantry lands went ahead under the pretence of religious zeal. Prayers for the souls of the dead were declared 'superstitious', so St. Andrew's lost much of its income and land in the process.

Valuable church furnishings came under the same rule. As a result, in 1547 the churchwardens sold monumental brasses from graves, and all the "Altars, Images and superstitious things in the church were removed". The following year the rood was taken down, and the churchwardens sold 1 cross, 1 censer, 1 chalice and more copper from the graves, for £27. The standing stone and wooden cross in the churchyard was sold for 9 shillings!

The church was 'whited' and painted with scripture sentences: the painted windows were replaced with plain glass. The high altar was replaced by a deal table with wooden benches on either side. Williams comments that "it must have seemed little better than the common-room of a tavern".

Each of the Inns of Chancery connected with the Church had for many years made contributions towards the upkeep of their chantry chapels or altars. When these were abolished, the lawyers began to make payments "in the name of their pews". It is reasonable to suppose that they were also instrumental in helping to retain the Thavie bequest, or at least that part of it relating to the fabric of the church.

All this upheaval occurred within the six years of Edward's reign. Then came a complete reversal, with the accession of Henry's Catholic daughter, Mary. The churchwardens then had to "erect and set up all manner of superstitious things again in the church, not long before pulled down". The written scriptures were scrubbed off the walls; a rood screen re-erected and the statue of St. Andrew re-gilded at a cost of 4s. 0d. To pay for all this, it was found necessary to levy a tax on the parishioners. Bentley seems to deplore their willingness to comply with the Royal Proclamation, but we all know the fate of those who refused. (Smithfield was put to a more sinister use at this time).

In 1556 the bells of St. Andrew's were rung "lustily at the quickening of Queen Mary with child". Sadly for Mary, she was not pregnant, but suffering from the malignant disease which was to cause her death two years later.

With the accession of Queen Elizabeth I in 1558 there was another religious 'U turn'.

Bentley was obviously delighted at the accession of protestant Elizabeth. He wrote, "In the first and second years of her Majesty, were all the altars and superstitious things in the church set up in Queen Mary's time, now again, to God's glory, pulled down, and by little and little all the relics of Rome utterly turned out of the Church".

The churchwardens may have been over-zealous, for they sold off more brass, defacing monuments in the process. This was contrary to Elizabeth's wishes, but it must have been common practice, because she had to issue two proclamations to try to stop it.

THE REFORMATION

Gradually the church was converted to the needs of the time. In 1568 a new organ loft with pews was built at the west end of the church, to house the 'great organs'. Unfortunately it was pulled down again three years later and the organs sold to Robert White, who had become Master of the Choristers at Westminster Abbey (his father had built the organs). Installed in Westminster Abbey, they were greatly prized; later churchwardens tried to buy them back, without success.

A new long form was made for communicants - the Communion Service was introduced here in 1564 - a so-called "removing" pulpit was installed, and a Venetian carpet was bought for the communion table. Various pewter and silver pieces of church plate were purchased, and several more books. The Bishop's Bible, a new translation, cost £3. 0d; this had to be displayed in church, chained, of course.

In 1578 the Royal Arms were set up in the chancel window: the new glazing had now been completed. Five years later, an explosion of gunpowder in the small Fetter Lane arsenal blew all the windows out again. We are told that they were quickly repaired.

In 1582 the middle aisle between Staple Inn and Barnard's Inn pews was paved, and nine new pews were built for the chancel. They contained 'benches, kneelers, leaners and doors'. The next year a new extending wainscot communion table was bought to match the 'new works'. At this time, too, the vestry was extended; it was provided with a chimney and its windows were re-glazed. For Bentley, replacing the lead roof with tiles was ' not the best husbandry'.

With all this refurbishing taking place, the churchyard seems to have been neglected, for in 1582 a heap of bones and skulls, lying 'unseemly and offensively' at the east end had to be gathered up and re-interred in a pot.

In 1587, under the rectorship of Richard Bancroft, the bells were re-cast and re-hung, and a clock was placed on the steeple. The list of subscribers to the cost of all this is an impressive one. Headed by the Earls of Southampton and Bath, Sir Christopher Hatton, the two Inns of Court and the four Inns of Chancery, there were 240 contributors altogether.

Here Thomas Bentley's chronicle ends. As far as we know there were no major alterations to the church for some years.

II. PEOPLE 1547 - 1687

Now we need to look at the social and political changes which took place after 1547, and some of the people of St. Andrew's who were involved in those changes.

At first, life seems to have continued much as before - Elizabeth decreed that the English Prayer Book was to be used in every church, and that everyone must attend church once every week or pay a fine. St. Andrew's obviously complied with these new rules; there is no mention of any church papists in the area, and wealthy parishioners still gave their positive support.

Richard Bancroft was appointed Rector in 1584. He was the first of many distinguished and able clerics to be given the living, which was then under the patronage of the Earl of Southampton. In 1585 the Earl's sister was married in their private chapel at St. Andrew's.

Elizabeth also brought poor relief under state control. A local rate was imposed, and the distribution of the proceeds entrusted to parish churches. The inhabitants continued to leave money or property to the poor, or certain sections of society. St. Andrew's still helps local people as a result of their bequests.

Bentley tells of three unwanted babies left in the churchyard in the period from 1570 to 1583. The first was a boy, christened Andrew Holborn; the two girls were named Aminita Andrea and Agara Zababilime. They were sent to Christ's Hospital in the usual way, but sadly both girls died.

HOUSING PROBLEMS

A proclamation in 1580 addressed the problem of overcrowding. Building on new foundations was forbidden in the City and within 3 miles of its boundaries. The population of London and other large towns had increased alarmingly. London had about 50,000 residents in the year 1500; by 1600 this

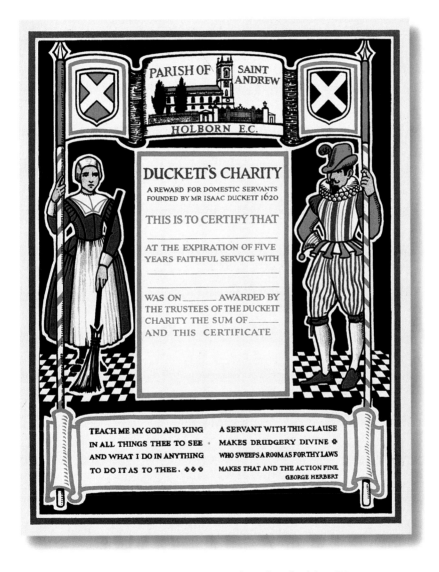

Duckett's Charity for domestic servants in the parish was founded in 1620

estimate had risen to 250,000, and was 500,000 by 1689. The Holborn area became urbanised.

Multiple tenancies of houses already in existence were the inevitable result of the Queen's ban on new housing, so a new law had to be introduced, to stop the practice of 'multitudes of families heaped up in one dwelling-house'. It was now forbidden to convert houses into 'such tenements'. This ban was largely ignored (in spite of the threat of imprisonment). In fact the one house and three shops left by John Thavie had become 13 messuages by 1600, and by 1686, 20 messuages. Whether these were all occupied by the 'very poor' mentioned in the proclamation, we don't know, but in the vestry minutes of the 17th. century there are frequent entries about tenants being in arrears with rent, and one or two dispossessions.

TOWARDS PURITANISM.

Richard Bancroft left St. Andrew's in 1597 when he was appointed Bishop of London, and eventually, in 1604, Archbishop of Canterbury. The next Rector was John King, another eminent cleric. He was a moderate protestant who seems to have had differences of opinion with his churchwardens - perhaps they were more puritan in outlook. However, he was Chaplain to James 1, who called him "the King of Preachers"! John King was appointed Bishop of London in 1611.

It was during the rectorship of Gregory Duckett that the Shoe Lane property was bought, it was said, from the Thavie Estate income.

In 1624, John Hackett was appointed Rector, and immediately set up a fund for rebuilding the church. Another moderate, he too had problems with the more extreme puritans among his flock. Lectureships had been established at St. Andrew's in 1570, and these preachers probably influenced churchgoers more than John Hackett did. He held two livings, St. Andrew's and Cheam in Surrey. He admitted that Cheam was for health; St. Andrew's for wealth (his stipend here was £300 per year). Accused of charging extortionate fees for christenings, weddings and funerals, he was exonerated, and the Bishop of London afterwards adopted his fee of 6s. 8d. for a parishioner's burial and 10s. for a stranger.

CIVIL WAR.

In 1642, soldiers drew their swords to attack Hackett in church when he was baptising a child. We are told that only "wisdome of some grave and able men of the parish" prevented too much harm being done. The following year he was questioned by the House of Commons Committee for Scandalous Ministers for alleged superstitious teachings. Then in 1645, Dr. Hackett was dispossessed, and his fund for the rebuilding of the church was confiscated. He did continue his ministry at Cheam, where he was able to use his beloved Book of Common Prayer without too much interference. After the Restoration John Hackett was appointed Bishop of Lichfield and Coventry.

Puritanism ruled; until 1662 there were no more Rectors at St. Andrew's; preachers were appointed by Parliament.

The Vestry Minutes betray no change of heart or of Government in 1660 except for one small item, "ordered - that there be a new Communion table made with Rayles of Wainscott rounde about it". The cost was £10.

Edward Stillingfleet was the next Rector of note, appointed late in 1665, the year of the Great Plague. Between May and October, 3,108 parishioners died. Everyone who could, left London, but the parish clerk of St. Andrew's stuck to his post - all the entries in the register of burials for the year are in the same handwriting. After the plague subsided, John Hackett, now Bishop of Lichfield, collected and sent £150 to help the poorer parishioners in their distress.

St. Andrew's escaped the Great Fire of 1666, and in 1668 Pepys wrote, "I to St. Andrew's Church in Holburne at the Quest House, where the company meets to the burial of my cozen Joyce; and here I staid with a very great rabble of four or five hundred people of mean condition and I staid in the room with the kindred till ready to go to church, where there is to be a sermon of Dr. Stillingfleet, and thence carry to Sepulchre's, but it being late, and indeed not having a black cloak to lead her or follow the corpse, I away, and saw indeed a very great press of people follow the corpse". Another entry in 1669, "And thence by coach to St. Andrew, Holborn, thinking to have heard Dr. Stillingfleet preach, but we could not get a place; and so to St. Margaret, Westminster....".   Nicknamed 'The Beauty of Holiness', Stillingfleet was much admired for his looks and personal charm. He was Chaplain to Charles II, but was not afraid to criticise him when necessary. Eventually was appointed Bishop of Worcester in 1689.

PARISH AFFAIRS

By now there were buildings 'adjoyning' to the Shoe Lane churchyard. One of the vestrymen was a builder. He asked the Vestry to inspect a property there to see if it were "any Nusance or prejudice to ye said Churchyard". He also agreed to re-build a house in Fetter Lane belonging to the church, for £115.

A few months later in 1676, it was agreed that a Mr. Allen "should make a doore out of Eagle and Child Alley into Shoe Lane Churchyard and drye Clothes there to pay 30s. a year so long as he shall soe drye Clothes". Widow Tanner was also given permission to do this in 1684. These trivial domestic concerns were discussed and recorded with as much care as other weightier matters. Certainly they are more interesting to read than the later prosaic entries of the 19th. century.

Although St. Andrew's had escaped destruction in 1666, it was by now in a very dilapidated condition. The entry in the Vestry Minutes of May, 1682, states "Wee whose names are under written having viewed the Parish Church of St. Andrew Holborn London do report there is a Necessity for ye rebuilding ye said Church, in testimony whereof wee have hereunto set our hands the day

and yeare above written

    Edw. Pearce   Edward Strong   John Longland"

A NEW CHURCH.

The church was rebuilt between 1684 and 1687, at a cost of £9,967, to the design of Christopher Wren. The details of its construction are to be found in the archives of St. Andrew's kept at the Guildhall. It is obvious that Wren took a personal interest in the rebuilding, in close collaboration with Dr. Stillingfleet and the Principal of Thavie's Inn. He also retained the tower at the west end of the church, adding another storey, and re-facing it with Portland stone in 1704. It is the largest of Wren's parish churches; though less ornate than some, it was considered to be "one of the finest galleried type of basilican churches in existence".

III. THE THAVIE ESTATE - 1547 - 1687

In 1547 the rents from the four houses not left for chantry purposes realised £3.16s.10d. These properties, one known as The Church House (formerly Le Andrewe Cross, Thavie's own house), and three shops, lay between the churchyard and Thavie's Inn.

During this period, the churchwardens resisted several attempts to confiscate the Thavie properties and land. Bentley records payments and legal fees for this purpose.

In 1574 the estate consisted of 20 messuages (dwelling houses), 10 Tofts (homesteads) and 6 gardens with appurtenances in the Parish of St. Andrew in Holborn. This was confirmed by deed poll in 1584.

In 1619: All that Messuage or Tenement with the Appurtenances and 3 shops then divided into 13 Messuages or Tenements with their

Appurtenances situate in the Parish of St. Andrew in Holborn then or then late in the several Tenures of the said Persons therein particularly mentioned, their Undertenants or Assigns.

And also all those three and twenty Rooms or little Tenements with the Appurtenances in which the poor Pensioners of the Parish aforesaid did live and inhabit together then or then late in the several Tenures or Occupations of the several persons therein particularly mentioned.

Together with a certain Yard or Backside then used and to several Tenements or Rooms belonging, together with a certain piece of land then used as part of the Churchyard. And all those three Tenements with the Appurtenances and a Tenter Yard with divers pieces of Land called Garden Plotts with the Appurtenances situate in Shoe Lane in said Parish. And all and singular Houses Outhouses and Hereditaments whatsoever to the said Premises belonging.

By 1621 the Church House was known as the Quest House, and the alley next to it as St. Andrew's Alley.

By 1686 the thirteen messuages mentioned in 1619 had been sub-divided again. They had become 20 messuages.

CHAPTER FOUR

Expansion and Social Development

I. CHURCH AND PEOPLE - 1687 - 1863

In 1689, John Moore became Rector of St. Andrew's. He was yet another eminent incumbent, who left after only two years, when appointed Bishop of Norwich and eventually Bishop of Ely. In the same year, John Wesley's father was ordained at St. Andrew's by the Bishop of London.

John Moore was succeeded by Dr. Thomas Manningham, a very distinguished preacher. He was also Chaplain to Queen Mary, (of William and Mary), and took particular interest in the welfare of the children at St. Andrew's Schools.

By now the churchwardens were considering " letting part of the North

The North Prospect of S.t Andrews Church in Holborn.

Churchyard to build on".Two parishioners had offered 2s. 6d. per foot, but nothing was decided until 1699. Then all the front of the north churchyard except '22 foot to be allowed for gates' was leased for 40 years at £24 p.a. -to build "15 foot deepe from out to out, and 19 foot high for ye Shop and Roome over it. To be flatt rooft and cover'd with lead with Railes and Ballasters. Every tenement to drip as ye Hill descends". This looks as though some attempt was made to ensure that the buildings would harmonise with the style of the new church.

CHURCH SCHOOLS

There had been a church school in the parish since the beginning of the century: by 1650 it was being held in the Middle Row Quest House. Now, in 1696, the first of the Charity Schools was founded, run by school Trustees, and funded by voluntary subscriptions.

Several church schools were founded about this time, and in 1704 the first of the Church Schools' Annual Festivals was held at St. Andrew's - 2,000 children attended. In 1721, new premises were acquired for the school. The building was a half-finished Wren chapel on the corner of Cross Street and Hatton Garden. Wren's stonemason carved 2 'charity children', a boy and girl in their school uniforms, and they were mounted on the wall of the school.

These original effigies are those now placed at the west end of the church - during the second world war they were 'evacuated' to Bradfield College for safety. There are also replicas on the wall of the old Hatton Garden building, though it is no longer a school.

1696·St Andrew's Holborn Parochial Schools·Hatton Garden·E C·1925

THE EIGHTEENTH CENTURY

Wren completed work on the tower in 1704, and some repairs had to be carried out on the vaults, but there was general satisfaction with the new church. The churchwardens were still having trouble collecting the four successive church rates which had been levied during the rebuilding period. Offenders were being threatened with legal action, and a 'Suplementall' rate was to be added to the fifth, "upon publick notice".

In 1700 the churchwardens decided that the sacramental wine should be claret, 'for the time to come'.

Dr. Henry Sacheverell was appointed Rector by Queen Anne in 1713. He was famous (or infamous, depending on one's religious and political views) for the 'malicious, scandalous and seditious' sermons he had preached at St. Paul's and elsewhere. As a result, his impeachment and trial in 1710 had led to near-riots, and he had become something of a folk hero. He was forbidden to preach for three years after the trial, but Queen Anne may have sympathised with his High Church, Tory beliefs, for she appointed him to St. Andrew's immediately the ban was lifted.

One of a set
of Sacheverell
"playing cards"

Without Concern he from his Coach alights,
To Stand a Tryal which its Hearers frights.

Sacheverell was a rich man (through marriage!) and one of the first things he did was to pay the outstanding bills owed by the churchwardens for the Harris organ which had been built in 1699. It was said that the organ had been "shut up" since its installation, because of non-payment. However, 'Dotted Crotchet', writing in the 'Musical Times' in 1905 didn't believe this. He said that a contemporary writer had commented on the 'very fine organ', and surely would have mentioned the fact that it was silent and unused. But now two eminent musicians were to be attracted by the Harris organ.

The first of these was the organist and composer Daniel Purcell (brother of Henry), appointed in 1715. He died two years later and was buried at St Andrew's. In 1726, John Stanley became organist at the age of 12. Blind from birth, he could perform any piece after hearing it once. This gifted man stayed at St. Andrew's until his death sixty years later. He was also 'Master of the King's Musick': his cantatas and organ voluntaries are considered to be among the finest compositions of the eighteenth century.

Three important stained glass windows were fitted at the East end of the church at this time. The Price window of the Last Supper and the Ascension was greatly admired by most people, including Boswell. However, tastes change, and George Godwin wrote in 1839 that "as a work of art the window is not deserving of commendation". The other windows depicted the Royal Arms of Queen Anne, and the Arms of John Thavie. The latter was probably paid for out of the Thavie Estate.

The eighteenth century was to be a fairly settled time for the church: the daily services and twice-weekly evening lectures were well attended. The Elizabethan law that everyone must worship at least once a week was still in force, but by now the area was densely populated, so it must have been impossible to implement it. In any case, the parish was too large, and too diverse in character to accommodate all its parishioners. In 1706 the residents around Queen Square decided to have a Chapel of Ease of their own. Dedicated to St George the Martyr, it went on to be consecrated as a parish church in 1723. It was the first of five parishes to be created over the next 140 years. Holy Trinity, Little Queen Street (1829 - 31); St Peter's Saffron Hill (1830 - 32); Holy Trinity, Gray's Inn Lane (1837 - 38) and St Alban, Holborn (1862), were all carved out of the ancient parish of St Andrew's.

Besant, writing about London, says it was "a city filled with dignified merchants all getting rich, and with a decorous, self-respecting population of retail traders, clerks, craftsmen and servants of all kinds, a noisy but a well-behaved people. A church-going, sermon-loving, and orderly people". He then describes the other side "which presents the vice and sin and misery which always accompany the congregation of many people and the accumulation of wealth". He was talking of drink, and particularly of the cheap gin which became the opiate of the lowest underclass yet seen. Hogarth's "Gin Lane" was no exaggeration, it seems. 'Drunk for a penny; dead drunk for two-pence' was an advertising slogan of the distillers. So perhaps it isn't a coincidence that two of the most shocking incidents in St Andrew's history happened at this time.

In 1715 an entry in the vestry minutes, "Ordered that whereas Thomas Abraham late grave digger of this Parish hath been detected of several misdemeanours committed by him in his office as robbing the dead and other enormities by him most sacreligiously practised wee therefore discharge him from his said employment".

Dr Sacheverell died in 1724. He was buried under the altar of St. Andrew's Church, but in 1747 an article appeared in the 'General Advertiser' which must have horrified the residents of Holborn, "John Lamb, Sexton of St Andrew's Church, Holborn was committed to Newgate by the Lord Mayor for being concerned with the grave-digger in stealing 150 lead coffins out of the vault of the said Church, several of which were found in his house. Among the leaden coffins taken out of the vaults, are found those of the late Rev. Dr. Sacheverell and the noted Sally Salisbury". According to a three-penny pamphlet printed after the trial, Lamb, and Bilbey the grave-digger were quite unrepentant. Lamb enjoyed a party the night he was sent to Newgate, and said that many others had done the same, and worse. One question, if asked, doesn't seem to have been answered; what had they done with the bodies?

Even the Parish Clerk invited trouble in 1718, when he accepted a bribe of £5 to tear leaves from the marriage register so that William Godyard might marry a second wife while his first was still alive. They were both pilloried as a result!

If moral principle was 'totally destroyed amongst a vast body of the lower

Lamb and *Bilby* robbing the Dead in the Church Vaults.

ranks', punishment was harsh and brutal. There were 48 offences punishable by death; 19 offences merited transportation, imprisonment and whipping; 21 more were punishable by whipping, pillory, fine and imprisonment.

No wonder the vestrymen, churchwardens and parsons of the day were kept busy trying to help the growing numbers of needy poor. They also had to administer 19 charities by 1830 (exclusive of the Thavie Estate). The records of their efforts are among the thousands of St. Andrew's documents held at the Guildhall. Distribution of the Government's supply of cheap coal and wheat to the poor was also their responsibility, as was the running of the workhouse in Shoe Lane. In 1795, the addition of having to 'raise by vestry' 14 men for voluntary service in the Navy must have caused a few headaches!

In 1722, a retired sea-captain, Thomas Coram, apparently saw newly-born children 'left to die, on the dung-hills in and around London'. This so infuriated him that he decided to do something about it. He had to overcome apathy, opposition and many other difficulties, until his dream of a Foundling Hospital was realised seventeen years later. The first admittance of children to a house in Hatton Garden was in 1741, and later the Foundling Hospital was built. The tomb of Thomas Coram was moved to St. Andrew's when the church was re-built in 1961, together with the organ case from the hospital:. Handel was said to have donated it in 1750. The pulpit and font also came from the hospital.

Above: Coram's Tomb.

Below: William Marsden

Another man of rare social conscience was William Marsden, a young surgeon who found a young woman dying on the steps of St. Andrew's in 1827. He was unable to get her in to any hospital and she died. Against the advice of his fellow-doctors he opened a Surgery in Greville Street for the poor and destitute, and eventually founded the Royal Free Hospital in Gray's Inn Road (now in Hampstead) and later the Royal Marsden Hospital.

The church-yard at St Andrew's was

officially closed for burials in 1720, though we know that it continued to be used. There was also the Shoe Lane "pauper's" burial ground, and now a new burial ground churchyard just off Gray's Inn Road was bought. In 1824 the City Corporation wanted to create a new Fleet Market on the site of the Shoe Lane burial ground and workhouse. After three years of negotiation, some land of the adjoining Bangor Estate was available, so the ground was consecrated by the Bishop of London, and the original site sold. The 17th Century bas-relief sculpture of the Resurrection which had been over the entrance of the Shoe Lane burial ground is now set in the north wall of the church.

The state of the churchyard was so bad that it prompted a letter to The Times from 'anti-pestilence' in 1841. He said "as respect the mound of mortality surrounding St. Andrew's Church, it is of the most abominable description. I remember some years ago it became necessary to rebuild part of the wall surrounding the mound in front of the Church, and as I was passing by it at the time it was unmasked, the effluvium arising from it was such that I ran past it with the greatest precipitancy, and could scarcely get rid of it during the whole day".

FAMOUS PARISHIONERS

Three minor poets of the Eighteenth Century had been buried at St. Andrew's during this period. John Hughes (1720), Thomas Chatterton (1770) and Henry Neele (1798). Chatterton committed suicide at the age of eighteen. Many of his contemporaries praised him rather extravagantly - Wordsworth, Southey, Byron, Coleridge. Keats dedicated 'Endymion' to his memory, and Dante Gabriel Rossetti wrote a sonnet to him.

Charles Lamb's mother and father were buried here, too, in 1796 and 1799 and his "Aunt Hetty". In 1808, Charles was best man at the wedding of his friend William Hazlitt, and Mary Lamb his sister, was bridesmaid. Lamb wrote to a friend, "I was at Hazlitt's marriage (in St. Andrew's Holborn) and had like to have been turned out several times during the ceremony, anything awful makes me laugh".

Another notable wedding was that of Marc Brunel in 1799. He was the engineer of the first tunnel under the Thames, and the father of Isambard Kingdom Brunel of Great Western Railway and Clifton Bridge fame.

Henry Addington, first Viscount Sidmouth, was baptised here in 1757. He became the Prime Minister who was unfavourably compared to Pitt

> "Pitt is to Addington
> As London is to Paddington"(Canning)

Another Prime Minister to be, Disraeli, was baptised here in 1817, aged 12.

In 1837 Dickens wrote 'Pickwick Papers' while living in Furnival's Inn. In 'Oliver Twist' Bill Sykes refers to the clock on St Andrew's tower, and Saffron Hill is supposed to be the location chosen as Fagin's den. Looking at engravings of the area at that time, it is easy to see why. The workhouse in Shoe Lane may also have been an inspiration to him. A churchwarden earlier this century went through the old parish registers, and found over 40 surnames used by Dickens in his books - if there really was a Mr Heep, he can't have been very flattered by the use of his name!

For a factual description of this part of London in the mid-nineteenth century, 'Mayhew's London', edited by Quennell, is unique. Reading it, we understand why it was necessary for the parsons and curates of the day to be accompanied by plain-clothes policemen when on pastoral visits to certain districts.

In spite of all this, St Andrew's was determined to maintain standards, and spent £7,041 on extensive repairs and refurbishment in 1818 and 1819. Then, in 1824 a further £2,572 went to rebuild the Inquest and Vestry rooms in St Andrew's Court. Yet more church repairs were carried out in 1832-3, costing £1,423. The Thavie Estate income was clearly inadequate, so money was raised by mortgage to pay for these improvements.

Before moving on to the greatest upheaval so far in St. Andrew's long history, we ought to look at the state of the parish in 1829. The Reverend Edwin Bedford, writing in 1929 - a hundred years later - was unusually critical of the church in general and of St. Andrew's in particular. He quotes a prominent writer of this period "No attempt was made to meet the spiritual needs of the largely increased populations in town parishes, and education was only within the reach of a small number among working classes".

The Rev. Gilbert Beresford, Rector of St. Andrew's in 1829, took his clerical duties lightly, according to Edwin Bedford. "He by no means preached every Sunday, very rarely took a baptism or wedding, unless in the case of some well-to-do parishioner". During that year there were 1,288 baptisms, 346 weddings and 587 burials. "The Curate's time must have been almost entirely taken up with baptising, marrying and burying the parishioners and their children all days in the week! There is nothing to show the size of the congregation on Sundays, nor is the number of the communicants given, even on Festivals, while week-day services were a thing unknown".

In defence of the Rector, it should be noted that St. Andrew's was one of the largest and most densely populated parishes in London (it had not yet been sub-divided). The Industrial Revolution had brought about changes that most people found difficult to understand and come to terms with; no wonder the clergy were slow to respond to their changing needs.

As for education - St. Andrew's continued to support the two parochial schools in Hatton Garden, and clothe the children where necessary. It helped them to obtain apprenticeships where possible, when they reached the age of fourteen, but it was impossible to provide for every poor child in the parish.

Shown on pages 46 and 47: London from Clerkenwell 1753. St Andrew's is in the left middle ground with St Bride's beyond.

II. THE THAVIE ESTATE (1825)

Under Thavie's Will:-

No 63 Holborn Hill, a messuage with shop and appurtenances

No 62 Holborn Hill, formerly 2 houses

No 60 Holborn Hill, a messuage

No 59 Holborn Hill, a messuage

No 58 Holborn Hill, a messuage

No 57 Holborn Hill, a messuage

A messuage in St Andrew's Court, leased to John Pontifex

A house in St Andrew's Court, leased to Richard Wells

A house in St Andrew's Court, "in which the Rector resides rent free"

A building lately erected on the site of a back -house, formerly part of No 63 Holborn Hill consisting of:-

    A basement occupied as a dwelling place by the sexton

    Ground floor, two apartments - one used as a vestry room, the other as a sexton's office.

    First floor, a large room with an anti-room, used for general parochial and ward meetings

Under the purchase deed of 1615:-

The workhouse in Shoe Lane, leased to Richard Pitt

A house adjoining the workhouse on the south (leasehold)

No 39 Shoe Lane

No 40 Shoe Lane

The Shoe Lane properties were sold for the Fleet Market project for £9,500, and a further payment of £4,500 was made for part of the Bangor Estate equal in size to the Shoe Lane burial ground: a total of £14,000. The Bangor Estate was then purchased by the Trustees for the same amount.

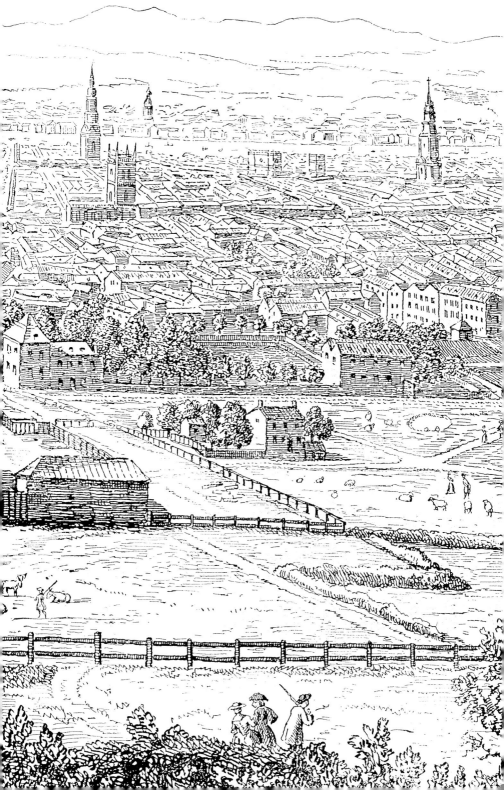

CHAPTER FIVE

Adjusting to Change

I. CHURCH AND PEOPLE 1863 - 1941

By now, the Fleet river had been vaulted over, and Farringdon Street created in its place, but this did not solve the problem of the two hills; one on either side. Holborn Hill, in particular, was so steep that it was dangerous, not only for horses trying to pull heavy wagons and buses, but for pedestrians, too.

So it was decided to build a viaduct over this 'valley', which would link Newgate Street with Holborn at the end of Hatton Garden. At the same time, the Corporation planned a new road that would run from the Hatton Garden end of the viaduct down to a widened Shoe Lane, thus connecting it to Fleet Street, and Farringdon Street.

The Holborn Valley Improvement Scheme went ahead. In the process, St. Andrew's lost most of its north churchyard, and all the church lands to the west, and to the south. The Rectory and Quest House had to be demolished, as well as other properties. Queen Victoria opened the Viaduct in 1869. It had cost £2.5 million.

Before the construction could begin, the north and west churchyards had to be cleared. It is estimated that between 10,000 and 12,000 'bodies' were removed to the Ilford City Cemetery, where they were re-interred in a mass grave with a single memorial stone. This operation cost the Corporation just over £12,000.

We really must pay tribute to Henry Blunt, the Rector, the churchwardens and the trustees for their tenacity in trying to get adequate compensation for the loss of land and property. The original offer of £35,000 was refused - they went to Court and the jury awarded £36,000. Again, when the Holborn Valley Improvement Additional Works Bill came into force in 1867, they made sure that the Corporation paid for alternative accommodation (for the Rector and Parish Clerk etc) until the new Rectory and Courthouse were built. Their request that the Corporation should provide a site for these buildings was refused, however, so the south churchyard was chosen, and S. S. Teulon was invited to draw up plans. His fee was 150 guineas, and the Corporation agreed to pay £10,000 for the new buildings, exclusive of special foundations. The south churchyard was now cleared of bodies (a further £2,000 or so) and the result we can see to-day.

Below: Teulon's "Gothic" Courthouse

Here, another small mystery emerges. Teulon incorporated in his new Courthouse a magnificent early 17th Century overmantel, black with age and filthy through neglect, which we are told came from 'The Questhouse'. St. Andrew's had two Questhouses; one in Middle Row, the other in St. Andrew's Court near the church, so from which one did it come? A local historical society maintains that it had been in the Lower Liberty Questhouse - the one near the church - but facts seem to suggest otherwise. Both Questhouses were demolished at this time; all the old houses in Middle Row were pulled down because they obstructed the flow of traffic along Holborn. The Upper Liberty Questhouse had housed the old Court Leet, sheltered corpses in their coffins before burial, and had been used as a schoolroom. The house was well described "... and above stairs, on the first floor, one large and spacious room, call the Quest Room, well-floored and lighted, with several coats of arms in the window, the walls well wainscotted or panelled, also a fair chimney-piece of wrought (or carved) wainscot over the fireplace, which doth much adorn the room." The Lower Liberty Questhouse, on the other hand was only fifty years old, and when it was built there was no mention of transferring a chimney piece from the old building. Wherever it came from, we can imagine the surprise and delight of Henry Blunt and the others when it was restored to its original glory in the new Courthouse. It is still there to-day - a delight to us all.

Teulon also 'improved' the church. He removed the organ gallery and case; installed a new organ; altered the Sanctuary; removed the old box pews and the christening pew; replaced the old windows with tinted glass, and decorated the church "with polychromatic ornament" in turquoise, stone, vellum, white, silver gray, indian red and gilding. Wren had covered up the ancient west window and closed up the great Gothic arch that connected the church to the tower, but now Teulon exposed them again - probably the only good "improvement" he made. Most people agreed with Bumpus when he wrote that he "ought never to have been allowed to touch a church of this kind". Looking at photographs taken later, the overall impression is of over-ornate gloom.

Interior of the Chuurch after Teulon 1876

The work of the church continued. By 1882, repairs in the Court House were needed, and some alterations made. There was no shortage of money; the proceeds from the Holborn Valley Improvement were invested in Consols (3%) until suitable property investments could be found. The Lodge was now built at a cost of £221, initially for the use of the curate.

Meanwhile, the carving-up of the old parish meant that changes had had to be made in the distribution of the income from the other charities concerned, and the approval of the Charity Commission obtained. It was all very complicated.

In 1890, the number of Trustees looking after the Thavie Estate was increased to 9, plus the Rector and two churchwardens in an ex-officio capacity. In 1892 the Thavie Estate became the St Andrew Holborn Church Foundation. The occupations of the nine are given as - an undertaker, a hotel keeper, a bookseller, a silk and linen draper, a distillery manager, a printer, an upholsterer, an optician and a silversmith.

This list reflects the changing 'face' of Holborn, which was becoming more and more commercialised. The outcome of this was that the resident population fell from 2,883 in 1881 to 2,269 in 1896: a decline that would continue for another fifty years; many people who were evacuated during the Second World War never returned to the city.

In 1894 the Rector, Henry Blunt, became ill - very ill indeed. (So did the Curate in his little Lodge, but this was only mentioned in passing!) We are not told the nature of his illness, but it led to a very thorough investigation of the drainage system, which was found to be 'defective', (a classic understatement!) £333 was spent on repairs and the Rector recovered, much to everyone's relief.

By the end of the century, St. Andrew's had become just another parish church. Now deprived of its prominent position at the top of Holborn Hill, hemmed in on all sides by tall buildings, and with only a tiny strip of garden on the Holborn side much lower than the pavement, it must have appeared diminished in size and in importance. But in "The City Churches" by the Rev. H. W. Clarke, written at this time, the evidence is all of prosperity. A detailed description of the expenditure for the year 1897 is given, and Clarke is very critical about the extravagance of some of the items mentioned. He seems to have been particularly concerned that the Rector received £30 a year for repairs to the parsonage and courthouse, whether it was "expended or not on such repairs". He also states that "the average annual expenditure for fabric and divine worship is about £1,300" and that "the Rector or churchwardens or parishioners have no anxiety whatever in providing this enormous annual income".

Henry Blunt died in 1899. The next incumbent was the Rev. Dacre Craven. In 1905, the organ was reconstructed: the Lord Mayor, Sheriffs and Aldermen attended its "re-opening". With nearly 3,000 pipes being blown by hydraulic power, it was a source of pride to the parish.

Sydney Pitt became joint parish clerk with Marshall Pontifex in 1907.

In 1915, many of the men of St. Andrew's went to war. The Rector's two sons were mentioned - one was a Lt-Colonel in the Royal Horse Artillery - the other a Lt. Commander in the 'Grand Fleet'.

The Rev. Edwin Bedford was appointed Rector in 1917. An erudite, kindly man, his hands-on approach and involvement in parish affairs made him an ideal incumbent for the years between the two World Wars. It was the era of 'In Town To-night' and 'Children's Hour'; open fires and crumpets for tea. The monthly parish magazines of the Twenties and early Thirties are full of the activities of Girl Guides and Rangers, Scouts and Cubs, the Old Scholars' Association, Women's Sewing Circle, Jumble Sales, holiday excursions et al.

In all this, Edwin Bedford had the active support of his wife. Margaret Bedford was a remarkable lady - we shall hear more of her later - and her help was invaluable during the 'Depression of the early 30's'. Their son, Felix, reminiscing about his boyhood days at St. Andrew's remembered how often he encountered strangers on the back stairs - "Mother's lame ducks".

The church bells were re-cast and re-hung at the end of the first world war, and in 1932 the church was re-furbished after an appeal for funds by the Rector. No other major works are reported during these years.

In 1937, Mr Bedford retired, and the Rev. Russell Howden was appointed early in 1938. The following year, when war was declared, the already sparse congregation was depleted even further by conscription and the evacuation of civilians to safer areas. The church and vicarage suffered slight damage in October 1940, but on the night of April 16th 1941, during a week when 100,000 incendiary bombs were dropped on London, St. Andrew's received a direct hit. The interior of the church was completely destroyed, yet incredibly, the walls and the tower still stood. A letter written in 1950 (the signature is illegible) says, "I can well remember watching the blazing ruins, while the firemen looked on helplessly, with only a trickle of water dripping from their hoses".

St Andrew's ablaze after fire bombs
April 16th 1941

II. THE CHURCH FOUNDATION ESTATE 1893

Rectory House in St Andrew Street.

Court House in St Andrew Street.

Vestry Clerk's Office No 16 St Andrew Street.

Shop on south side of Holborn Viaduct and north and west sides
of St Andrew's Burial Ground, No 31 Holborn Viaduct.

The freehold messuage known as No 24 Haymarket.

The freehold property known as the Wandsworth Common Estate
comprising 16 houses in Morella Road, 15 houses in Thurleigh Road
and 5 villas in Bolingbroke Grove.

Also various amounts of money invested in Consolidated stock
for purposes defined by the Charity Commissioners.

I. THE WAR AND POST WAR PERIODS
1941 - 1965

This could have been the end of the St. Andrew's story. So many city churches had been damaged or destroyed that it would not be possible to rebuild them all. In any case, some had already become "surplus to requirements", and therefore redundant, according to many people.

Margaret Bedford had other ideas. The widow of the previous Rector was now living in retirement with her brother, near Basingstoke. Charles Letts, an ex-churchwarden of St. Andrew's wrote to her six days after 'the calamity' (his own words) detailing the damage. He said, "the interior of the Church has been utterly destroyed. The only part of the furniture which remains is a portion of the stone pedestal of the pulpit. The roof is no more. The tower, however is standing and the bells are I believe untouched. The walls of the church still stand and ten of the pillars which supported the galleries also remain. The Rectory and Courthouse were not damaged ... the Communion Plate was all saved and also the registers. The safes in the Verger's Vestry are all right. There is another matter relating to the loss of the Church which I do not think advisable to put in a letter but I will tell you all about it when we next meet." Here, Mr. Letts may have been referring to the Crypt. The bomb, or bombs, had blasted through the floor of the nave, and the crypt was now a jumble of coffined remains (some of which had burst open) and rubble, filling the entire space up to the arched ceiling.

Mrs Bedford was in no doubt. St. Andrew's should be re-built - must be re-built. She wrote to anyone and everyone who might be influential. The replies to some of her letters over the next five years, 1941 - 1946, have survived, and they show Mrs Bedford's determination to keep a high profile for St. Andrew's in spite of a growing opinion that many of these old churches had outlived their usefulness.

In 1944, the Bishop of London wrote, "I fully recognise the historical value of St. Andrew's, and you may be perfectly certain that when we do come to reorganisation, we shall have that very much in mind. I know you must be anxious to know what the final outcome of all this will be, but we can only bid you be patient as we all must be, and to have good hope that the right thing will be done".

The Bishop's interim report (1944) stated as a matter of principle:- "that no Wren Church, not already destroyed, nor damaged beyond the possibility of satisfactory restoration, should be removed ... and after all the schemes for entire or partial preservation have been fully considered".

Two years later the final report of the Bishop's Commission was issued. Eleven churches were to be rebuilt or restored: St. Andrew's was said to be "capable of restoration, has a strong parochial life, and is the outstanding representative amongst the City churches of the evangelical tradition" (The Times, October 22 1946).

Mrs Bedford must have been very happy when she heard the news, but the 'new' church was to be very different to her vision of a restored parish church. The list of reasons why St. Andrew's should be re-built, which she submitted to the Commission, now seems quaintly old-fashioned in outlook - not even politically correct perhaps, but it does reflect the spiritual and moral beliefs of her generation. Looking back, the lady's efforts - fund raising, chivvying the authorities - may not have had much influence on the Commission's decision, but they certainly stand as an example of the loyalty and devotion that St. Andrew's has inspired in quite ordinary people over the centuries.

Meanwhile, the Rev. Russell Howden and church officials had carried on their work with the few parishioners that were still in the area. The Courthouse was used for services, and the St Andrew's charities continued to be administered by the various trustees. In 1943 the War Damage Commission agreed to pay £14,593.0s.5d in compensation for the loss of the contents of the church, but no amount of compensation could replace, for instance, the magnificent porphyry altar given to Dr Sachaverell over two hundred years before, or the eighteenth century stained glass.

There were other financial difficulties. Some of the Church Foundation properties had also suffered from enemy action, particularly the Wandsworth estates. This resulted in a considerable drop in income.

II. ST ANDREW HOLBORN
BECOMES A GUILD CHURCH

By the City of London (Guild Churches) Act of 1952, the Bishop designated St. Andrew's as a Guild Church. No longer viable as a parish church, it would now "be available for worship ministrations and religious instruction to the non-resident population of the City..." Each such church should be in the charge of a Clerk in Holy Orders who in addition to his fitness to minister to the non-resident population of the City, should also possess special qualifications in scholarship, preaching, pastoral work or administration or other particular qualifications which render him suitable to offer specialised ministrations or services under lawful authority elsewhere."

So the new Guild Church of St. Andrew would have a vicar with no parochial responsibilities as such, but who would have other diocesan concerns, allocated by the Bishop. The parish of St. Andrew now ceased to exist - divided between St. Brides and St. Alban's, but the incumbents of these parishes would have no jurisdiction over St. Andrew's, the Vicar, or any stipendiary curate appointed to assist him.

The rest of the constitution was fairly straightforward. There would be churchwardens (and Sidesmen if required) as before; a Guild Church Council; a Church electoral roll, and a Guild Church Clerk, who was to have Parish Clerk status. The freehold of the church and churchyard were now vested in the Bishop of London, and St. Andrew's would continue 'to be and belong to the diocese, the Archdeaconry and the rural deanery.' The changed status would apply, though the church was as yet un-restored: the emphasis on youth training and education was accepted in 1955, and this led to other changes in the use of the Vicarage and Courthouse.

A NEW APPROACH

It was generally accepted that a fifteen-roomed vicarage was no longer necessary - apart from the cost of heating and maintenance, so Seely & Paget produced a report in 1957 on how the accommodation might be modified. Ground floor rooms could be used as offices; the first floor and part of the second floor as a sizeable flat for the Vicar, and a one-bedroomed self-contained flat also on the second floor, which could be let. The work was completed in 1959, when the Vicar (now the Rev. Frank Hopkins) occupied the main flat, and a churchwarden, Miss Reynolds, the small top-floor apartment. The Youth Training Service was accommodated on the ground floor, and the London Diocesan Fund occupied ground floor rooms of the Courthouse. A firm of glass-makers, Hoskins Rose, were operating from the basement.

THE CHURCH FOUNDATION

The Parish Clerk, Mr Hewitt Pitt, of Pontifex Pitt, continued to administer the various charities from his firm's offices at 16 St Andrew Street, which they had occupied since 1871 (leased from the Church Foundation). In 1955 the City Corporation, who had provided this building as a replacement at the time of the Holborn Valley Improvements, decided to serve a Compulsory Purchase Order notice on it because it did not fit in with their plans for the area. They offered the site of 22 St. Andrew Street in exchange and this was approved by the Trustees. As in 1871, they were to have a new building - but owing to planning regulations then in force, it had to be a certain height, so No 22 would be one-third larger than the old premises. The Corporation therefore insisted that the Foundation (as freeholders) should grant the Corporation a 999 year lease of the ground floor and basement at a peppercorn rent, so that they could under-let them to recover part of their expenses. The Charity Commission sanctioned this transaction, and Pontifex Pitt moved to the new offices (on five floors) in 1956. Mr Hewitt Pitt resigned as Clerk to St. Andrew's in 1960, and was succeeded by his cousin, Mr Walter Pitt. The move was not to be entirely satisfactory for Messrs Pontifex Pitt, but for the next five years the administration would continue unchanged.

THE CHURCH

Re-building complete, the church was reconsecrated in October 1961. It had been restored "stone for stone and brick for brick", as the Commissioners had promised, to the original Wren designs, by Paget and Mottistone at a cost of £125,000.

As part of the restoration, a Lady Chapel was formed at the west end of the church. Its 17th Century English Baroque reredos came from the ruined church of St. Luke, Old Street, and its window was the work of Brian Thomas, a modern glass painter, who also created the window over the high altar. Other appropriate furnishings - the pulpit, font, and organ case came from the old Foundling Hospital in Bloomsbury. The tomb of its founder, Thomas Coram, was placed at the west end near the Lady Chapel. It is said that Handel, who was a friend of Coram, helped to design this organ, and gave recitals on it.

We wonder what some of the older residents of Holborn thought when they went into the 'new' church for the first time. The interior was now light, graceful and airy, if comparatively unadorned. Did they miss the old familiar Victorian "improvements" of Teulon? Whatever their views on this, one thing was certain. Everyone was thankful that at last the church was functioning again. There would be no more Sunday services, but the church would be open for public worship during working hours on week-days with lunch-time mid-week services, and special services (eg. Baptisms, marriages, burial and memorial services) could be held, with permission from the authorities. It was also hoped to hold concerts and suitable exhibitions, when possible, for this had been one of the aims of the Commission on the formation of Guild Churches.

The Rev. Roy Deasey became Vicar in 1961, but he resigned two years later and the Rev. David Manship was appointed temporarily as Priest-in-charge. Several important projects were pending, but these would not be realised until a new vicar was appointed.

Left:
The interior of the Church
after rebuilding.

Below:
St Andrew's House
obscuring the Church
from Holborn Circus
until 1967
when it was demolished.
A public garden
now stands on the site.

CHAPTER SEVEN

New Directions 1965 - 1981

The Bishop of London decided that St. Andrew's should be used as

a) the Headquarters for the Diocesan Council
for Voluntary Religious Societies

b) as a centre for Post Ordination training, and

c) Lay training

The Rev. Prebendary George Timms was chosen as the next vicar, to implement this decision.

Almost immediately, the effect of this appointment was felt in many ways.

CHURCH FOUNDATION

A new scheme was now in operation, and the accommodation in the Vicarage and Courthouse was re-allocated. A lease was granted to the London Diocesan Fund, who then sub-let to the London Diocesan Youth Service. In return for the lease, the L.D.F. paid £7,000 for Courthouse refurbishment. The training group still occupied two rooms.

Hoskins Rose had vacated the basement, and Miss Reynold's lease of the top floor flat was terminated.

By October of the same year, 31 Holborn Viaduct had been sold to the Corporation in part exchange for the head lease of the ground floor and basement of 22, St Andrew Street. The Church Foundation would now own the whole building, when the extra £5,000 (the difference between the £17,500 paid for 31 Holborn Viaduct, and the cost of the head lease at £22,000) was found. At the same time, a report on all the Church Foundation properties had been commissioned, and a decision was reached to sell the factory property at 18, Leather Lane in order to complete the above transaction with the Corporation.

RADICAL CHANGES

Pontifex Pitt did not take up their lease of the upper floors of 22 St Andrew Street until 1970, but in December 1965 Walter Pitt wrote to the Vicar in his capacity as Clerk to the Foundation and the other charities. It was a long letter, detailing the history of his family firm's association with St Andrew's since 1823, and it was clear that he hoped for preferential terms financially when the new lease was drawn up, as well as an assurance that his cousin, Gerald Griffiths, would take over his clerkship when he retired.

We have no record of the Vicar's reply, but it was not to be. When Walter Pitt announced his retirement in 1970, George Timms had already appointed James Holden as his Personal Assistant and Bursar of St. Andrew's Vicarage and Courthouse: in 1972 he took over the clerkships that had been held by Pontifexes and Pitts for almost 150 years.

Whatever the reasons for this major decision - and there are several possible explanations - the results were startling. The day-to-day control and running of the Foundation and other charities was now possible as the new clerk moved to the Vicarage; the administration was no longer the part-time responsibility of someone outside the Church.

The old Wandsworth properties were sold off during the next few years, making the Church Foundation comfortably solvent for the first time since the end of the nineteenth century, and this was only the beginning. Since then, the Foundation has gone from strength to strength.

In 1970, George Timms became Archdeacon of Hackney, whilst continuing as Vicar of St Andrew's. Offices were made available on the ground floor of the Vicarage to house the Archdeaconry staff, and in 1974 the Youth Service

group moved out of the Courthouse.

OTHER PROPERTIES

By this time Pontifex Pitt (now merged with Walker, Martineau) had vacated the upper floors of 22 St. Andrew Street, so they were leased to Comins & Co. The basement and first floor were still occupied by Boult, Wade and Tennent, but they left the following year, when a short lease was granted to Scrimgoers Ltd., pending negotiations with Comins & Co to take over the whole building.

The other large property owned by the Foundation, 24 Haymarket, was occupied by the Government of Malta (as sub-lessees) and the lease was due to expire in 1980. The Trustees were expecting to have difficulty in obtaining vacant possession when the time came to re-lease the property, so this subject was to dominate their meetings for the next five years.

CHAPTER EIGHT

Modern Times 1981-1998

When the Venerable George Timms retired to Kent in 1981, he was succeeded by the Venerable Roger Sharpley as Archdeacon of Hackney and Vicar of St. Andrew's, thus continuing the practice of combining the two posts. The Vicarage and Courthouse offices became the administrative centre for the Archdeaconry and lay training in the Stepney Area, whilst post-ordination training and other functions moved elsewhere. Jim Holden continued as Clerk to the Foundation with offices in the Vicarage.

The finances of the Church Foundation received a boost when the lease of the Haymarket property was sold during the boom years of the mid-eighties. This created a stability, which, for almost the first time, allowed the trustees to plan a programme of refurbishment for the Church and Vicarage complex and to consider how St Andrew's could best adapt to provide a positive community role.

THE ORGAN

The main gates were refurbished, and the pulpit re-gilded, then the proposal that a new organ should be installed was considered. Inevitably, there were arguments pro and con, but eventually it was agreed that the cost could only be justified if the organ could be fully utilised. Well, yes it could.

The new organ, completed by Manders in 1989, was built in a style influenced by the great English organ builders of the mid-nineteenth century - especially Gray & Davidson and William Hill. It was dedicated in October 1990. Six months later the Royal College of Organists moved its headquarters from Kensington to St Andrew Holborn, taking over the two large first floor offices at the West end of the church, and the basement of the Courthouse for use as the library. Members were now able to practice daily and the College had a fine organ for its examinations. And of course the organ was always available for services, concerts and recitals. The musical tradition of St. Andrew's was to be revived.

The new organ installed in 1990

Other works carried out during the latter part of the eighties included changing the boiler from oil to gas, redecoration of Coram's Tomb, electrical works and the refurbishment of the Courthouse basement. More recently the exterior stonework of the Church was repaired and 35 years of London grime removed, the tower clock and bells overhauled and the charity children figures outside the west door repainted.

Serious consideration was given to a scheme to excavate the crypt area as a shelter for the homeless, but eventually this idea was abandoned due to the enormous expense involved, not only in carrying out such a project but in the running costs needed to keep the shelter operational thereafter.

CHANGES AND NEW DIRECTIONS

The arrival of the Royal College of Organists in 1991 coincided with other changes at St Andrew's. Jim Holden, the Clerk to the Foundation died in July of that year, and was succeeded by the present Clerk, Ian Gray. Shortly afterwards Roger Sharpley retired as Archdeacon of Hackney and Vicar of St Andrew Holborn. His successor in both, Clive Young, took up post within weeks, an amazingly rapid transition in Church terms, perhaps demonstrating the importance of the duties involved.

THE MELLISH MONUMENT

Steady progress continued to be made on refurbishing the Church, Vicarage and Courthouse in recent years. Inside the church this included renovating the Lady Chapel, where most weekday services are held. The opportunity was taken to install a monument in the Chapel to William Mellish, a wealthy parishioner who died in 1699 and who was originally buried at St Andrew Holborn. After his death, his widow, Dorothy, moved to Nottinghamshire, where she died. Her Will stipulated that William's body should be taken north to be buried alongside hers in the churchyard of the remote country Church of St Leonard's at Ragnall. This little church, and a few forlorn cottages, stand as forgotten reminders of an earlier industrial age, amidst open, flat, pastureland on the Lincolnshire/Nottinghamshire border. St Leonard's became redundant in 1993.

A fine marble memorial plaque in St Leonard's commemorated the William Mellish story, and, as the future of the church was uncertain, it was decided that it would be appropriate to place the memorial in St Andrew Holborn and install it in the Lady Chapel as part of the refurbishment. This work was completed and the Chapel re-dedicated in 1993. It could be said that William Mellish came back to his roots nearly 300 years later.

The Mellish Monument in the Lady Chapel

At the same time a memorial tablet was commissioned from John Skelton in memory of Jim Holden, Clerk to the Foundation 1972 - 1991. This was dedicated by the former Vicar of St Andrew's, the Venerable George Timms on 23rd March 1994.

THE COURTHOUSE

The fine Courthouse by S.S.Teulon with its magnificent 17th century fireplace had been an unappreciated asset for many years and by 1992 it needed a thorough refurbishment. The trustees sought professional advice on appropriate ways of using the Courthouse as a more significant source of income and, as a consequence, an imaginative scheme was prepared to refurbish the main rooms so that the Courthouse could be used more beneficially as a venue for quality dinners, banquets, conferences and receptions as well as continuing to provide for the more traditional church and parish events.

The decorative scheme adopted for the Courthouse was based upon a high Victorian style similar to the treatment of the banqueting hall at Castell Coch, the Earl of Bute's gothic castle near Cardiff. The success of the venture, with the modernisation of the vicarage kitchens, led to ancillary rooms being redecorated in similar style for inclusion in the venue package. Today the Courthouse suite is in use most days and is marketed as "Court House Events". It is an increasingly popular location used by a wide range of organisations and charities, both local and national, who generally express their delight at the decor and facilities provided at this very convenient location in central London.

The interior of the Courthouse today showing the 17th century fireplace removed from the original Courthouse and the 1993 decorative scheme.

THE CHURCH FOUNDATION ESTATE 1998

The Vicarage, 5 St Andrew Street.

The Courthouse, 7 St Andrew Street.

No 22 St Andrew Street.

No 24 Haymarket.

Also various investments at the discretion of the Trustees as prescribed by the terms of the Governing Scheme of the Charity.

Between 1893 and 1998 properties at No 18 Leather Lane and Nos 16 to 18 Fitzroy Square were bought and sold.

CHAPTER NINE

The Future

The role of St Andrew Holborn Guild Church as a place of worship in the City is somewhat limited nowadays by its non-parish status and a diminishing residential community in the area. Services for local workpeople on weekdays form the basic pattern, but inevitably numbers at services are fairly modest. The church is open daily and attracts a steady stream of visitors, and others who come to pray or sit quietly. However, the use of the church by the Royal College of Organists as its headquarters is a development that has provided St Andrew Holborn with an identifiable role as a City church. Both the Foundation and the College regard this as a platform which could provide an opportunity to develop the church as a centre of musical excellence and a venue for concerts, recitals and other musical productions. The 650th anniversary Thavie celebrations in 1998, which include concerts being arranged and promoted jointly by both organisations, herald a confident future for St Andrew Holborn.

CHAPTER TEN

Conclusion

Since the implementation of John Thavie's will, there have been many people, of every class and from a wide variety of callings, involved in the administration of his bequest. Most of them were honest, with genuine concern for the survival of the church in accordance with the benefactor's wishes. This in itself is unusual - ask the Charity Commission how many of these old bequests have lapsed or simply vanished. Or read the chapter on "Losses of Charity Funds" in that definitive work by the late W. E. Tate, "The Parish Chest".

Charity Children Effigies at the West End of St Andrew's Holborn

The church of St. Andrew, Holborn has been cherished and supported over the last six hundred and fifty years by generations of trustees, officials, churchwardens, rectors and vicars and their wives. It has survived riots, revolts, religious upheavals, plagues, wars, economic booms and recessions and general wear and tear. The Thavie bequest, in the hands of good stewards, should ensure that it will continue to survive and flourish, not just as part of our architectural heritage housing other activities, but first and foremost as a consecrated church. For this is not the end of the story.

"Serve God - and be cheerful" (Rector Hackett's motto)

Margaret Troke 1998

Rectors of the Parish Church
of St Andrew Holborn

Roger	1269
Gladerinus	1297
Richard de Tadelowe	1320
John de Wemyngton	1322
John Mynoth	1330
Thomas de Cottingham	1343
Robert Gome	1343
John de Reynford	1352
Thomas Ocle de Hereford	1359
William Wynel de Wenlock	1359
William Cantrey de Wenlock	1362
Laurence de Radeford	1374
Richard Holme	1375
John Wayte	1383
Adam Foxlee	1383
Nicholas Bagge	1391
Roger de Walden	1392
Archbishop of Canterbury	
John Ikelyngton	1392

Richard Pauncefoot	1394
Robert Eltesley	1394
Hugh Sprot	1396
Peter Heton	1427
William Prys	1427
John Pygg	1430
Bishop of Ardfert	
William Lynford	1432
William Fallan	1432
John Dygon	1433
Gilbert Worthington	1439
William Green	1447
Ralph Gartsyde	1478
John Burgess	1531
Thomas Smithson	1536
Nicholas Burton	1541
Ralph Whylin	1559
James Proctor	1579
Richard Bancroft	1584
Archbishop of Canterbury	
John King	1597
Bishop of London	

Gregory Duckett	1611	Henry George Blunt	1858
John Hackett	1624	Dacre Craven	1899
Bishop of Lichfield		Edwin Bedford	1930
James Lambe	1662	J. Russell Howden	1938
John Taylour	1664		
Edward Stillingfleet	1665		
Bishop of Worcester		Vicars of the Guild Church	
John Moore	1689	of St Andrew Holborn	
Bishop of Norwich & Bishop of Ely			
Thomas Manningham	1691	Frank Hunter Hopkins	1956
Bishop of Chichester		George Boone Timms	1965
Henry Sacheverell	1713	*Archdeacon of Hackney*	
Geoffrey Barton	1724	Roger Ernest Dion Sharpley	1981
Cutts Barton	1734	*Archdeacon of Hackney*	
Charles Barton	1781	Clive Young	1992
John Luxmoore	1806	*Archdeacon of Hackney*	
Bishop of Bristol, Hereford			
& St Asaph			
Thomas George Clare	1815		
Gilbert Beresford	1819		
John Travers Robinson	1838		
Jonathan James Toogood	1850		

The Bells of St Andrew's Holborn

They rang their message of weal or woe
In the days of Romish pride:
They caught a gleam of the fires below,
When the Smithfield martyrs died.
They rang for feast, and they rang for fast:
They rang for the Roses twain,
Ere the Red Rose scattered, and fell at last,
In the mire of the Barnet plain.
And lo, They rang for a mite to-day,
Who chewed at his fist the while,
Or wriggled about with his arms at play,
And a quaint little, toothless smile!
In years to come, you will understand,
And blush at the honour done -
They rang for Warwick the Kingmaker;
and they rang for YOU, my son!

They rang at first over stream and dell
Where the nodding alder shook,
And toilers bowed to the vesper bell,
As they rowed on Turnmill Brook;
When Ely's lord had a fair demesne
With chapel and gatehouse, too,

And Saffron Hill was an upland green
Where the purple saffron grew.
They rang the obit of bishop and priest:
They rang for His Majesty's grace,
When Henry rode to the serjeants' feast
In the hall of Ely Place.
The same old bells -in the same old tower,
good sooth, as records run!
They rang for King Hal and Queen Katherine;
and they rang for YOU, my son!

Pealing and tolling from year to year,
They hailed the centuries through,
Hero or sovereign, abbot or peer
Ere ever they rang for you -
You, such an image to favour the joke,
Fidgetting there on your spine,
Such a hot little shrimp in the christening cloak
Your grandmother thinks so fine!
Sucking a fist that is pudgy and soft,
Working your bonnet awry,
Deaf as a post to the clamour aloft,
Though the great bells clash on high;
All Holborn astir with their music;
And you such a figure of fun -
They rang for the Nile and Trafalgar;
And they rang for YOU, my son.

From "Rambles with an American"
(pub Mills & Boon)

Bibliography

Hustings Rolls, Letter book E
City of London Record Office
Catalogue of letter books, ed. Sharpe
Guildhall Library
Catalogue of Coroners' Rolls, 1300 - 1372
Guildhall Library
The Bentley Register of 1584 (MS4249)
Guildhall Library
Vestry Minutes 1651 - 1706
Guildhall Library
Minutes of Trustee Meetings 1860 - 1922
Church Foundation Archives
Minutes of Church Foundation Meetings
1941 - 1991
Church Foundation Archives
The City Churches Interim Report 1944
Church Foundation Archives
City of London (Guild Churches) Act 1952
Church Foundation Archives
Bedford Correspondence (letters 1941 - 1946)
Church Foundation Archives
Lamb and Bilby (Pam 9463)
Guildhall Library
Discovering London's Guilds and Liveries
J.K.Melling (Shire Publications 1995)